Endocrinology

Mei-mei Berssenbrugge

poetry

Kiki Smith

art

Kelsey St. Press 1997

Publication of this book was made possible by grants from the National Endowment for the Arts and the California Arts Council.

First Edition

Library of Congress Cataloging-in-Publication Data

Berssenbrugge, Mei-mei, 1947-
        Endocrinology / Mei-mei Berssenbrugge, poetry; Kiki Smith, art.
        1st ed.
                p.   cm.
        ISBN: 0-932716-41-5 (alk. paper). – ISBN: 0-932716-42-3 (Limited
        edition with a signed Sugarlift Color Etching on Kitakata; alk. paper).
        1. Body, Human–Poetry.   2. Body, Human, in art.   I. Smith, Kiki.
        1954-.   II. Title.
        PS3552.E77E53   1997   97-20715
        811' .54–dc21   CIP

Book design by Kiki Smith and Robert Rosenwasser
Produced by Rena Rosenwasser

Kelsey St. Press, P.O. Box 9235, Berkeley, CA 94709
Tel: (510)845-2260   Fax: (510)548-9185
Email: kelseyst@sirius.com   Web: http://www.sirius.com/~kelseyst

for Barry and Richard

I

The bird watches the man and woman dance.

Tongue

He touches her stomach.

There's circulation around her in intercapillary space, empty or hollow, in relation to organs.

A virus transfers firefly genes to a tobacco plant.

The plant glows in the dark.

Shoulder

How much evolution derives from "something in the air," not a square of light above a niche in a white wall.

Light, your intestines. Fluid, lines of light.

As if, when you think about something, it already has a frame that's a priori.

Think before that moment, freedom is inside there.

Think before the man and woman, their freedom of the animal among silvery trees.

Mold

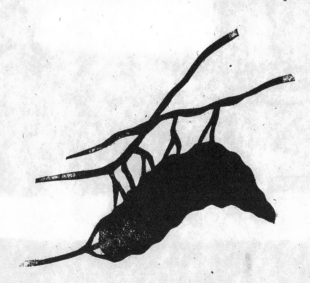

Which trunks the light hits is an endocrine permutation, a state of being or a physical state.

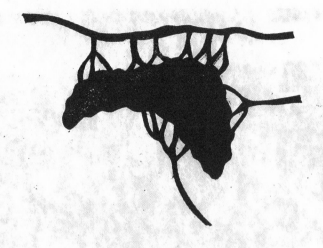

Innocence

Hormones are molecules, material, invisible.

Their flow is random, mesh through which the body is sensed, not an image.

The form of her body is important, as how she is here, though there's no physical evidence of her physical suffering.

II

Hormones provide a mechanism by which the body relays chemical signals through cells perfused by blood.

There's a structural need to make tectonic episodes which might otherwise become pliant.

Hair Line

Conceiving of the body as a space of culture tends not to refer to it as nature, unless it's been taken away by disease,

hairy ears, genital ambiguities like a shamanistic object, not generic.

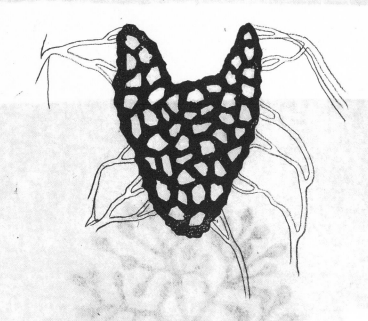

fat

Because she's in a body, it makes decisions.

Black rock in a dry river, weeds tangled at its base, something heavy enmeshes with something light.

The material, of non-negotiable contingency, the feeling, a different structure on different physical levels.

grease

A pool in the forest gleams with organic matter, its depth of the possibility of imbalance in the body,

when luminosity detaches itself from feeling as emanation, transparency, a structural need to become disorganized.

What is physical light inside the body?

A white cloth in a gold and marble tomb, to focus the expression of the tomb.

Shortly after phagocytosing material, leucocytes increase their oxygen consumption and chemically produce light.

going out with a
string
on the other side

During pregnancy, the foetalplacental unit under the curve acts as a gland.

If the mother is diabetic, the foetus becomes her mother's endocrine system.

This occurs in all animals whose circulations are linked.

skin of the head

Osteoclasts of an irradiated animal derive from the marrow of its parabiont.

Later also, their systems associate like writing, knowing edges of a system and areas in-between, an outpour of molded sand with iron rocks in crevices, as in a story she accepts not knowing if her lost child is alive.

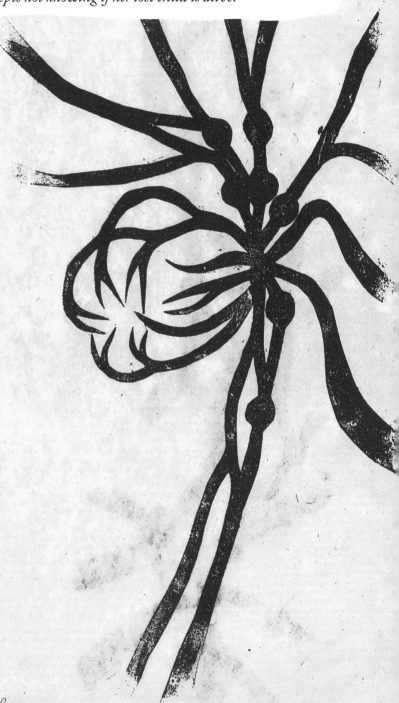

Nothing

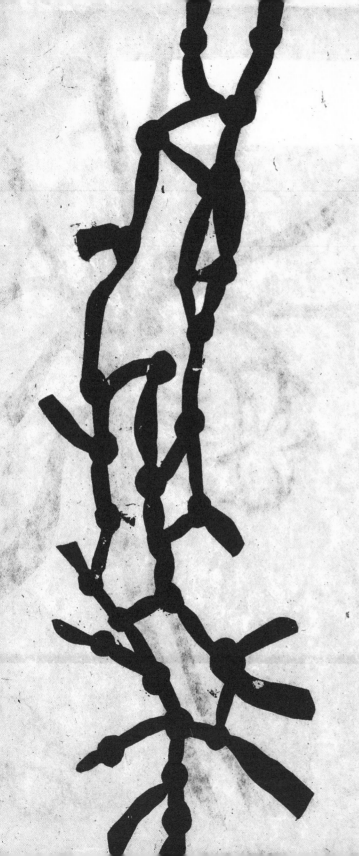

spinning on a pivot

11

III

The bird sings on a strawberry the size of a melon.

Cells release hormones into intracellular space, where they enter local, fenestrated capillaries.

A bird eight feet tall with disproportionately huge claws and beak.

The woman, moon-faced, hair grows from her, and she feels desire for the man touching her abdomen, that feels like love.

Prolactin in our bird induces nestbuilding.

Bowl

Estrogen induces her concept of his luminosity, detaching itself from his color.

Her hands enlarge.

She can't see where her sadness ends and someone else's is.

falling Backward

The line between chemical and emotion is the horizon inside a niche in her body, transferring non-being to utility.

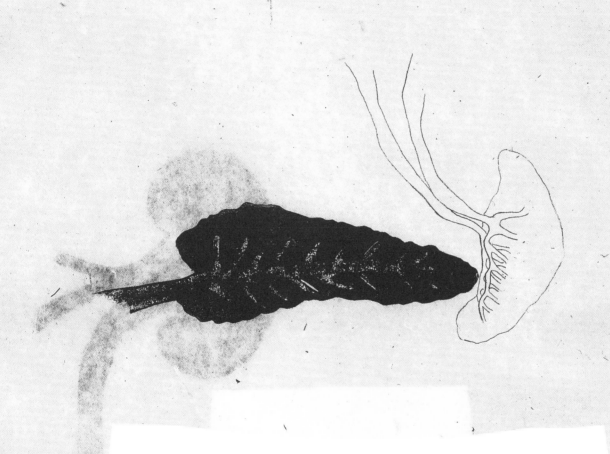

She lives on moisture from dew condensed on soil surfaces from night air.

The strawberry sprouts a fantail of petals.

glory

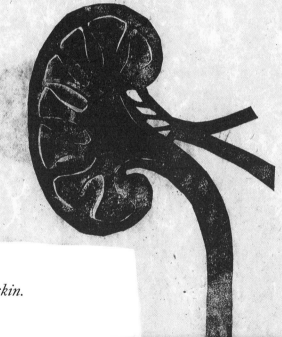

Air flames on her skin.

She believes the body, though densely saturated, is generic, dreaming the same nightmare as the child.

His presence triggers latent feeling beyond feeling for her, with enormous affection for her body.

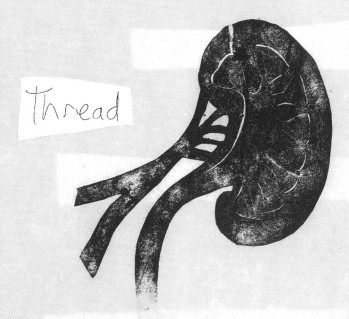

Thread

Blood drips under a white feather of the wounded bird.

A vein puts the organ in the background.

She concentrates on manipulating her organs to pull the white square of light precisely into the niche.

IV

The woman leans on the table, forearms abnormally long.

Her milk flows and flows. She cries and cries.

These are unaccountable imperfections in the numerical fabric, not mysteries.

A wire crosses in front of a line on the wall, while its shadow seems to cross behind it.

Blood over the arm

The place where a word originates in her body is the physical source of her sense of beauty,

so you can change the word for "happiness" that was formerly, "innocence."

Inside the rib

The respiratory system when stimulated produces a characteristic sighing.

The thymus expends itself during stress and collapses, so an autopsy finds only a membrane.

resignation

Touching a wall produces the sound of touch on another wall.

Feedback between health and fate unfolds so fast,

there's no way one step in the chain can be based on the previous one.

Center

An associative smear or aura requires her to be in a body, in order to make decisions.

Lack of cloud cover causes thermal energy on the desert to return rapidly to the sky at night.

Oxygenating molecules makes light.

Lighting the organs, they turn white.

He loved her body as much as he loved her as an individual.

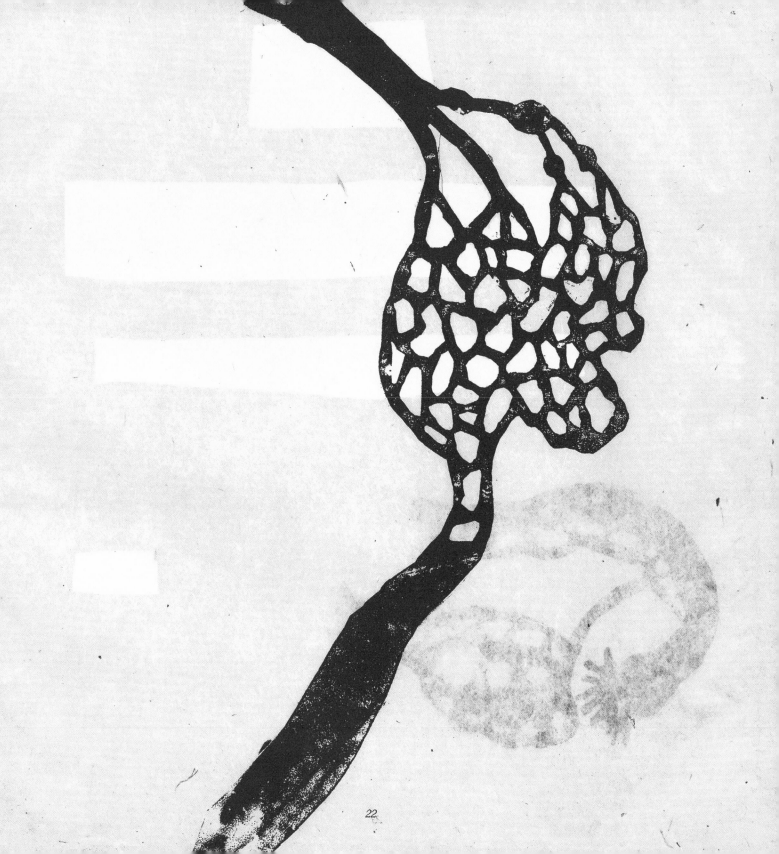

V

There is a space.

You see something at the far edge, and your eye going over this space makes a whole, like watery mass in a gourd,

the feeling of old organs no longer crucial to or inside themselves,

while remembering people you loved, which flowed from the physical, about which you made decisions.

Man

To make this whole, any object, brings into being something not in nature, an interior measurement, yourself,

not yourself, bursts of growth when you sleep.

Her back bleeds.

Zero

A spray of blood on the snow.

She sits on her hands physically preventing herself from scratching.

Peeling away

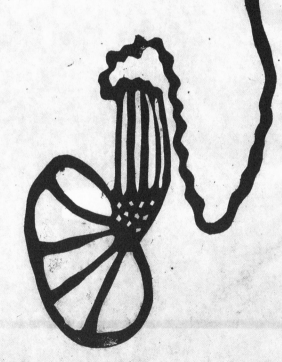

The child, her sense of the world being crucial to or inside itself, of memory and specificity, like script.

B cells grow for years in a petri dish.

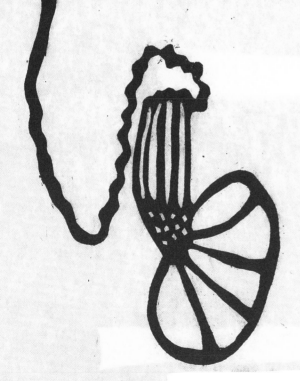

Shaking in two different directions

The sick, immortalized cells don't know to stop growing.

Where your eye goes over space to the horizon makes a whole, but where sky meets the earth,

the fragment is not the same as a whole.

Desert ferns covered with reflecting hair may insulate the fronds.

Silver

Radiations of a state barely embodied, then dissolving in counter-reflections of light.

There's an engine.

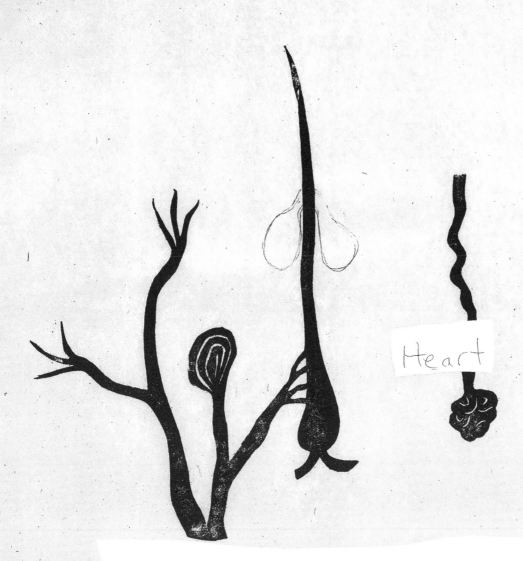

Heart

He cannot separate from the loved person, to shed the loved body.

Mei-mei Berssenbrugge was born in Beijing, China in 1947. Her books include The Heat Bird *(Burning Deck),* Empathy *(Station Hill Press), and* Sphericity *(Kelsey St. Press). She lives with artist Richard Tuttle and their daughter in New Mexico, where this collaboration took place.*

Born in 1954 in Nuremberg, Germany, **Kiki Smith** *resides in New York City. She is an artist who works in a variety of media. Her art has been featured at the Österreichisches Museum für angewandte Kunst, Vienna; in* Projects *at the Museum of Modern Art, New York; and at the Musée des Beaux-Arts, Montreal. She is represented by Pace-Wildenstein Gallery.*

Endocrinology *is a limited edition of two thousand copies;*
sixty, numbered, signed by the artists,
with an original Sugarlift Color Etching on Kitakata paper.
The text face is Caslon Book Italic.
Printed at West Coast Print Center on Mohawk White Superfine.
Foil stamp on Graphika Chip Gray Cover.

In its original form the work was produced by
Bill Goldston at Universal Limited Art Editions, Inc.
This edition evolved from transparencies of the original book.

Design by Kiki Smith and Robert Rosenwasser
Kelsey St. Press 1997